DESTINATION
CALIFORNIA

At Fisherman's Wharf in Monterey, the atmosphere of John Steinbeck's "Cannery Row" still lingers.

DESTINATION
CALIFORNIA

Photographs: Christian Heeb
Text: Gunther Barth

WINDSOR BOOKS
INTERNATIONAL

Bizarre sinter deposits at Mono Lake. For the last fifty years, Los Angeles has been tapping four of the seven rivers flowing into the lake.

CONTENTS

The Golden Gate Bridge, built between 1933 and 1937, is San Francisco's principal landmark.

CALIFORNIA: ALMOST AN EARTHLY PARADISE

The Magic of Water

The first, brief mention of California in Western literature was also the first tribute to the unique character of the region. In 1510, the Spanish novelist García Ordóñez de Montalvo wrote: "To the east of India lies the island of California, which is almost an earthly paradise." Having implicated Queen Calafía of California in the adventures of his hero Esplanadián, the writer quickly redirected his attention to the siege of Constantinople, which must have seemed quite mundane by comparison with his fictional vision of life in California.

Over the centuries, the notion of California's uniqueness was repeatedly confirmed by eyewitness accounts. Following its discovery in 1542 by Juan Rodriguez Cabrillo, a Portuguese navigator in the service of the Viceroy of New Spain, tales and rumours multiplied concerning the splendours of the region. The publication, in 1865, of the first-ever geological survey of California did nothing to dispel these legends: if anything, it lent added weight to the accounts by giving them the authority of scientific opinion. The survey proved, in scientific terms, that the beauty and grandeur of California were the products of unique natural circumstances.

The physical appearance of California is determined by water, and also the lack of it. It is a land of droughts and floods; the state's political boundaries accord exactly with the geographical limits of the only region in North America which has both winter rains and summer dryness. The importance of water immediately impresses itself on first-time visitors who see the various shades of green and brown dominating the landscape. In many cases, this initial impression is shaped by the dryness of summer rather than by the damp, snow-freshened green of the rain-soaked winter. As soon as the floods recede and the sun has dried up the remaining traces of the winter rainstorms, the prevailing colour of the landscape becomes a dull summer brown.

The brown of mid-summer begins to emerge in the spring, wherever there are no sea mists or alpine snow reserves, no rivers, streams or irrigation channels to prolong the survival of the winter green. The grass quickly takes on the colour of the parched soil, whose surface, cracked and rutted by the sun, is ground into a whitish-yellow dust by the incessant winds. But although the range of California's colours is limited, these pale, sun-bleached tones are continually cited as the yardstick of natural beauty, even where they are obscured by evergreen shrubs and trees, by irrigated fields and meadows, and by the artificial green of the cities and towns.

It takes some time for the newcomer's eye to discover the golden California of travel agency brochures in the scorched brown of the grass or the ash-grey of the bone-dry soil. But little by little, one reaches the conclusion that the typical colour of the region is indeed gold, rather than grey or brown. This realization is partly prompted by the colour of the golden poppy, the flower which was declared the official emblem of the state by the California Senate in 1913. The golden poppy, which at one time grew wild all over the region, symbolizes the sunshine and the mineral wealth of California. It was given its botanical name, *eschscholtzia californica*, by the German writer Adelbert von Chamisso in honour of a surgeon who was a member of the 1816 Russian expedition led by Otto von Kotzebue, to what was then the northernmost province of the Spanish-American colonial empire.

Ever since the first discovery of gold at the site of a sawmill on the American River in 1848, the story of the Gold Rush has been the dominant myth of California. Prior to this, however, the element which held the most potent fascination for the Californian imagination was·water. If magic there be, it is in water that the true magic of California resides. Before the arrival of the first Spanish settlers, one of the most arid parts of southern California was inhabited by the Gabrieleño Indians. One of their legends tells the

Union Square, in the heart of downtown San Francisco, has a rather special geological location. Positioned directly over the [...]'s main fault, [...] dynamic area [...] destroyed by a 1906 earthquake. Now the street features some of the [...]'s finest shops and hotels.

story of a coyote who proudly regarded himself as the world's freest and most independent creature, freer even than man himself, but who was forced to acknowledge the miraculous power of water. One day, he came to a sluggishly-flowing stream and rashly decided to challenge it to a race. He ran along the bank as fast as he could, but after a time, he became completely exhausted and collapsed; as he lay by the stream, the water continued to flow past in front of his nose.

This mystical reverence for water was common to all the original native inhabitants of California. As citizens of a nation which was still in its infancy, the white Americans from the north grafted their own romantic nationalism onto the myth of water: they saw the rivers and lakes of America as the natural features which mode the United States the finest country in the world. Early travel diaries were filled with both awe and admiration of the canyons and waterways of the American southwest.

For some time, the magic of water was supplanted in California by the myth of gold, and although the gold fever of the nineteenth century played an important part in hastening the economic development of the state, it also destroyed valuable parts of the landscape and seriously upset the balance of the relationship between man and the natural environment. In the race to get rich quick, mountains were levelled and valleys filled, rivers were redirected or drained, and entire forests were chopped down to provide wood for pit-props in the mines and to build houses for the gold-diggers.

When the gold ran out, it seemed for a moment that California was doomed, as a ruined paradise at the edge of the continent which had been robbed of its riches and suddenly abandoned. However, the disastrous reign of gold was outlived by the magic of water. Water enabled industry and agriculture to flourish, and it still continues to work its everyday miracles in the teeming cities and lonely villages, in fertile fields, thriving orchards and tranquil gardens. Several of the region's most popular sports are connected with water: canoeing down mountain rivers, for example, or power-boat racing on the reservoirs. More and more Californians are rediscovering the magical powers of water, and some of them are beginning to see it as a resource which is just as precious as the fertile soil that feeds them, or as the air which, despite the pollution, is still eminently breathable.

A nostalgic reminder of the hippie era: button-sellers on a street-corner in San Francisco's Haight-Ashbury District, where the Flower Power Movement which swept the world in the 1960s originated.

However, a large number of Californians continue to regard water as a kind of liquid gold, a substance which can be used at will to transform deserts and wastelands into orchards and fields as well as land for housing, paying no heed to the disastrous ecological and cultural consequences which ensue when the resource is misused. Despite the constant interventions of man, the availability of water heightens the impression that the California landscape contains a natural abundance of all the elements necessary to satisfy the material demands of an ever-increasing population.

The illusion of California's uniqueness is also nurtured by the exceptional variety of its landscape. The valleys and mountains, fields and forests, cities and desert enable Californians to pick out the images in agreement with their own personal vision of the Promised Land, fitting them together like so many pieces of a jigsaw puzzle. The California myth is infinitely flexible: it is open to all and can be adjusted to suit anyone's individual requirements. California appears as varied as the Garden of Eden, as fruitful as the Promised Land, with a wealth of scenic contrasts which is additionally amplified by the state's sheer size.

From Deserts to Gardens

Following Alaska and Texas, California is the third largest state in the Union, with an area of 158,693 square miles (411,013 square kilometres). It extends over nearly ten degrees of latitude, from the 32nd to the 42nd Parallel, which roughly approximates to the boundaries of the Mediterranean. The westernmost point of the state is also the westernmost tip of the United States' continental landmass. As the crow flies, the distance from north to south is about 750 miles (1200 kilometres), and the journey from the northwest to the southeast border is as long as that from The Hague to Naples, travelling via Paris, Bern, Milan and Rome. At its widest point, the state extends over 260 miles (420 kilometres), which is approximately the same as the distance between Brussels and Berlin; but in the narrow central region, only 160 miles (250 kilometres) separate the Pacific Ocean from the Sierra Nevada Mountains.

Hence the landmass of California is almost as large as the area occupied by France or Spain. Even in the age of jet travel, the state still has a mysterious aura of remoteness, dating back to the days when it was indeed largely sealed off from the outside world.

There was little contact between California and Spain or Mexico, and even after joining the Union, the state maintained its isolation for nearly twenty years, until 1869, when the completion of the Pacific railroad overcame the physical barriers, the deserts and mountain ranges which had separated California from the rest of the United States.

The Sierra Nevada Mountains, extending nearly 450 miles (725 kilometres) along the border between California and the neighbouring state of Nevada, is one of the mightiest ranges in North America. They are like a solid wall of granite, a barrier erected by nature to protect something precious and fragile. To the south, the range adjoins the Mojave and Colorado Deserts that themselves form a natural border between California and Mexico. The barrenness of these desert wastelands is almost beyond belief, and one soon wishes that the mountains, sand plateaus and salt-pans would disappear, and that a simple leap back into the familiar scenery of the green and pleasant coastal region could be possible.

Here, in the strip of land along the Pacific Ocean which was also a desert until its transformation, by irrigation, into a thriving land of orchards and gardens, the fundamental contradictions of California become particularly apparent.

In the shadow of Los Angeles, flourishing cities are interspersed with tracts of wasteland. Luxury abounds in the midst of poverty. The green waves of the sea lap at the pristine white sand, while the poisonous yellow smog, generated by the exhaust fumes of countless cars, rises to blot out the sun, creating a wholly artificial horizon, an unwelcome by-product of human technological ingenuity. As is so often the case in California, these contrasts largely result from the crowding of such a large population into a relatively restricted space, where the conflict between nature and culture is aggravated by man's total dependence on technology.

Following the transitional phase in the taming of nature, when the countryside was domesticated by planting fields, gardens and orchards, southern California acquired a largely man-made landscape, consisting of freeways, airports, bungalows, shopping malls and skyscrapers, in addition to the well-known symbols such as Disneyland, the Santa Anita Park racecourse or the Huntington Library and Art Gallery. Here, the future has already arrived. Taking its cue from the warped visions of Hollywood, southern California pursues a lifestyle in which things are often grotesquely out of proportion. This obsession with size and scale serves to disguise the sense of uneasiness which ensues when the normal relationship between the present, past and future is disrupted. Over the last hundred years, California has lived in a continual spiral of prosperity, with one sudden economic boom following another, and it cannot resist the temptation to flaunt its achievements in a way that no one can overlook. Even a simple event such as going to church is blown up into a spectacle which appears, and is, larger than life. Here, people not only drive to mass on Sundays: at the drive-in cathedrals, vast palaces of steel and glass, they actually sit in their cars for the duration of the service. The futuristic architecture of the church directly incorporates the car, which in California is an indispensable necessity of everyday life, into the religious spectacle, whose dimensions are overwhelming.

Southern California society adapted itself to the automobile with particular alacrity and soon devised a corresponding set of norms and rituals, such as the ceremony of Dad handing over the car keys when the kids turn sixteen, while a new driving licence allows instant access to an amusement park on wheels. However, the liberal, forward-looking attitudes of the region are combined with a traditional, conservative element. People are always looking for something to cling to and will seize on anything seeming to offer a form of security, be it the panacea of drug-induced illusions or the dubious certainties of a narrow-minded puritanism in turn lacking the consolation of genuine belief. Southern Californians derive a certain comfort from the success of their efforts in shaping the world about them, drawing on the experience of generations and aided by modern technology and a highly efficient administrative apparatus.

Over the last few decades, the multiplicity of contrasts in the south has come to be equalled by those in the north. On the periphery of the Bay Area around San Francisco, established urban communities with cultures which, by Californian standards, are positively ancient, have been overrun by rapid population growth and technological progress. The resulting tensions, exacerbated by the extreme contrasts of wealth and poverty, have led to sudden outbursts of violence: brought to mind, for example, are a millionaire's daughter who became involved in the guerilla activities of a make-believe army, and the collective suicide of the Jim Jones sect in a South American jungle clearing in Guyana.

Despite the dramatic changes of recent years, the northern part of the state, excepting Sacramento and the area around Lake Tahoe which have also been infected by the southern California lifestyle, has almost succeeded in retaining the character of a nat-

In parts of
[dow]ntown San
[Fran]cisco, relics
[of] the Golden
Twenties,
such as the
[Vesuvio] Bar on the
corner of
[Colum]bus Avenue,
[stan]d alongside
examples of
[ul]tra-modern
[a]rchitecture.
[Th]e skyscraper
in the back-
[g]round is the
[Tr]ansamerica
Pyramid, the
[h]eadquarters
of a major
[corpor]ation whose
[activ]ities include
[bankin]g, insurance
[an]d air travel.

13

Predating the earthquake and fire of 1906, the Victorian façades of the houses on San Francisco's Alamo Square.

urally unified entity. The range of mountains separates the north from the Pacific. And the ocean parts at the Golden Gate, the entrance to San Francisco Bay, one of the world's most impressive natural harbours.

Between the coastal mountains and the Sierra Nevadas lies the Central Valley, whose character is shaped by California's two major rivers, the Sacramento and the San Joaquin. Originally, the valley was a monotonous expanse of parched grass and yellow sand; following the transitional phase when the first fields and pastures were laid out, the region flourished as an agricultural centre and has now become a veritable horn of plenty.

In the spring, the smell of the hot asphalt on the freeways mingles with the scent of pear and almond blossoms, while the air itself is filled with billowing clouds of fragrant dust. When autumn comes, the flurries of sand and exhaust fumes on the misty horizon herald the arrival of the tractors as they work their way across the fields, preparing the ground for the seeds which will provide next year's crop.

The Long Road to Cosmopolitanism

Within a mere hundred years, California has passed through an evolutionary cycle with five distinct phases of economic activity. The naked exploitation of the region's mineral resources was replaced by simple forms of agriculture and industry which reduced the dependence of the gold-hungry population on imported goods. After the completion of the transcontinental railroad in 1869, a colonial phase followed which continued until World War II: during this period, which was marked by the emergence of industrial monocultures in mining and agriculture, California's main economic role was that of a supplier of raw materials to the manufacturers on the East Coast. From the 1920s onwards, the growth of the aircraft and shipbuilding industries, massively boosted by World War II, enabled California to develop its own manufacturing base. However, this trend was halted in the 1960s by the advent of the post-industrial society: nowadays, the state's prosperity is largely based on service industries such as trade, banking, insurance and real estate, and on the multitude of other activities in the private and public areas of the tertiary sector.

Unlike the economy, the varied landscape of California is a world unto itself. The region is like a paradise, albeit one which teems with contrasts, not only in respect to the landscape, but also in terms of ethnic and cultural diversity. All the races and most of the world's nationalities are gathered in California, and the population comprises a large number of different communities. The cosmopolitan character of the state dates back to its very beginnings, long before the Gold Rush, when the Spanish, Russian and British fleets first took control of the harbours and anchorages on the Pacific Coast.

In the post-1848 boom period, wave after wave of immigrants came to California from the eastern states of the Union, from Europe, Latin America and the Far East. Huge new cities with ethnically mixed populations grew up almost overnight.

It would be interesting to know the exact ethnic composition of the current population, which totals around thirty million. Unfortunately, no accurate figures are available which might reveal, for example, precisely how many people of British origin or descent are living in California today: despite the recent upsurge of ethnic awareness, the published statistics are based only on rough estimates. However, although they ignore the subtle differences between groups and sub-groups which have merged to such an extent that their distinguishing features are barely perceptible, the official figures do provide at least an approximate general picture. According to the most recent survey, published in 1990, the ethnic distribution of the population is as follows: fifty-seven percent European-American, twenty-six percent Hispanic, nine percent Asiatic, seven percent black, and 0.5 percent native Indian.

The Californians of Spanish-Mexican descent, many of whom also have Indian blood, form one of the state's "classic" minorities. In many cases, families can trace their origins back to the early days of the Spanish settlement towards the end of the eighteenth century. The 1830s and 1840s saw the emergence of a group known as the "Californios", whose members were either California-born or had lived in the region for so long that they had ceased to identify with Mexico, their country of origin. At this point, California was still a Mexican province, but in 1848 it came under the control of the United States; subsequently, many of the Californios were driven off the land which they had previously occupied, and their numbers and importance dwindled.

However, the upheavals attending the Mexican Revolution of 1911, coupled with the continual need for cheap labour on the big farms, led to a new wave of immigration from Mexico. Although the Mexican community grew rapidly in size, its social standing remained low: many of the new immigrants settled in the so-called *barrios,* a term which in Spanish simply means "quarter" or "district", but which in California

Salt deposits at Devil's Golf Course in Death Valley. The vast expanse of salt, formed by the evaporation of a saline lake, is entirely devoid of vegetation. With temperatures frequently topping the 50°C/132°F mark, Death Valley has claimed the lives of many travellers.

parlance denotes the ghettos and neighbourhoods of the Spanish-speaking population.

By 1945, Los Angeles already had the largest Mexican community outside Mexico City. The proximity of Los Angeles to the Mexican border was a stimulus to immigration, and since the 1960s, the ever-growing Mexican-American minority has played an increasingly important part in the political, economic and social life of the city and the state as a whole. The Hispanics have acquired a new sense of group identity: they bear their Spanish surnames with pride, and the Chicano farmworkers have staged a number of successful strikes against exploitation by agricultural employers.

The Indians are one of California's fastest-growing ethnic groups. When the first Spanish settlers arrived in the region, fifty years before the final collapse of the Spanish empire, the Indian population totalled about 300,000. Its members had been so successful in adapting to natural conditions in the various parts of California that the population density here was far greater than anywhere else in North America.

In the decades following, the Indians were quickly driven off the land by the white settlers and decimated by disease and poverty. By 1913, their numbers had been reduced to 17,000. However, the birth-rate began to rise again in the 1920s, and this factor, coupled with Indian immigration from other states of the Union, has led to a fourfold increase in the Indian population over the last sixty years. About ten percent of the Indians live on reservations, the largest of which is Hoopa Valley Reservation in Humboldt County.

The Chinese and Japanese communities constitute a kind of aristocracy among the Californian minorities. Their high status is based on their links with countries having long and venerable histories and whose political and economic importance has massively increased in recent years. For several decades, however, these Oriental minorities were regarded with open hostility by white Californians, who treated them with a mixture of outright brutality and scarcely-veiled legal discrimination. The workers' unions were afraid that Chinese labourers would depress wage levels, and the farmers' unions saw Japanese settlers on the land as dangerous competitors. In the early decades of the twentieth century, the Japanese were continually persecuted by the whites, who feared that California would fall prey to Japanese demographic conquest.

Over the two hundred years of California's history, minorities of widely varying sizes have repeatedly been used as scapegoats by the dominant political, economic and social groups or classes seeking to further their own interests or to add to their own prestige by persecuting others. Hypocrisy has often been accompanied by naked brutality: the prime instance of this in the recent past was the treatment of the Japanese community during World War II, when almost all of California's Japanese-Americans were interned in inland camps and stripped of their wealth and property.

To a certain extent, the development of California reflects that of the United States as a whole, albeit on a scale which is truly Californian. In addition to the Indians, blacks, Jews, and a wide range of European national or ethnic groups, all of whom, at one time or another, faced the hostility of white America, California has sizeable minorities from Latin America, China, Japan, Korea, the Philippines, India, Armenia, and recently, Vietnam.

Thus the uniqueness of California is partly founded on the diversity of its residents. The region contains almost every imaginable variant of race, ethnic allegiance and social class, with an exceptionally broad range of religious and political viewpoints. At first glance, it might seem that Californians have little in common, apart from the conviction that their earthly paradise is a better place than any other in which to live and work. This is the belief which originally drew many of them to the region and which has led to immigration on such a scale that every tenth American now lives in California. Between 1900 and 1990, the state's population rose from one-and-a-half million to approximately thirty million, and California surpassed New York in 1962 as the most populous state in the Union.

Within the space of a few generations, the differences between the various groups making up the California population often become blurred to the point of virtual extinction. In some cases, the distinctions are only maintained by legal definitions which classify a person with one Indian grandparent as an Indian, or a child with a Japanese father and a white mother as a member of the Japanese minority. However, despite the lingering elements of racial prejudice which are inherent in categorizations of this kind, both the "Indian" and the "Japanese" child count themselves as Californians. At the same time, they take pride in their status as members of communities which nowadays insist on being treated with respect, as a compensation for the discrimination of the past. Ultimately, all the minorities line up with the millions of people who regard the landscape, the development and the conditions of life in California as unique. One American writer was entirely accurate in his statement that Californians "are not just inhabitants of a state: they are a race unto themselves."

The Gathering Clouds...

The power of the California myth, which continues to casts its spell over so many people of widely varying origins, manifests itself most clearly in the sense of discomfort which ensues whenever one tries to reconcile the myth with reality. The population growth of the last few decades, reaching record levels in the 1980s when the population rose from twenty-four million to thirty million, is rapidly creating a new reality which has, in turn, made an impression on the California dreams.

The increasing size of the population imposes a massive strain on the economy and the state's social services. It also aggravates the continual problem of water supply: the demand for water is increasingly outstripping California's natural reserves of water, and the sheer number of the state's inhabitants is replacing the eternal cycle of drought and flood as the number one issue in water provision. This is bound to have severe economic, ecological and demographic consequences. Experts have estimated that, even in a year with normal rainfall, California uses more water than would fit in a channel two miles (three kilometres) wide and one foot (one-third of a metre) deep, running all the way from San Francisco to Washington, D.C.

The continuing water crisis has already begun to affect the structure of the California economy, which already has been hardhit by the restructuring of the American economy as a whole. Rising unemployment, declining output and cuts in state and community welfare provisions are a guaranteed recipe for social conflict. Since taxpayers have firmly resisted any attempt to raise taxation levels, the welfare system is on the verge of breakdown, and it has become impossible to overlook the steady increase in the number of homeless people.

These growing economic, demographic and social problems are gnawing away at the special status of California: the myth is on the point of being engulfed by a transformed reality. It is becoming more and more difficult to bridge the gap between legend and reality, to assemble feelings and facts into a coherent picture preserving the seductive image of California as a secular paradise.

... and the Lure of Gold

One of the main reasons why the California myth has endured for so long is that the unique natural landscape of the region seemed to echo human notions of the Garden of Eden. The Pomo Indians, a tribe which lived by the Russian River in the coastal mountains north of San Francisco, referred to themselves as the "Earth People", a name vividly conveying the closeness of their relationship with the land and the soil. This outlook was common to all the Indian peoples of California, who believed that their ancestors had originally sprung from the soil of their homeland. The Californios, descendants of the Spanish and Mexican conquerors, were also captivated by the magic of the landscape and themselves became a integral part of it. When the American trappers invaded the Mexican province in the 1820s and 1830s, they justified their actions with the belief that California was an essential natural part of the emerging nation which would soon extend right across the continent, from the Atlantic Ocean to the shores of the quite distant Pacific.

The discovery of gold in January 1848, only a few months after the occupation of the region by the American army, gave a particular boost to the new settlers' belief in the California myth. It seemed as though the gold deposits in the valleys and highlands of the Sierra Nevadas had been lying there waiting for the newcomers as a reward for their blind faith in the California dream. As soon as the first wave of fortune-hunters hit the region, the entire world fell under the spell of the California myth. Nineteenth century Chinese immigrants referred to the country of their dreams as the "Golden Mountain", while settlers from other nations expressed their hopes of overnight prosperity in similar terms.

In most cases, the dreams inspired by the gold mines failed to come true. A few prospectors did indeed find the ore and wealth they sought and quickly returned home; the example of their success encouraged others to persevere and brought a continual stream of new immigrants into the region. The sudden growth of the California population led to a general and massive increase in economic activity. In the new cities which sprang up almost overnight, the streets appeared literally to be paved with gold, and there were so many opportunities for earning easy money that the notion of the Golden West took on the status of fact, rather than fiction.

As it winds through Yosemite National Park, the Merced River offers one dramatic view after another, opening the visitor's eyes to the astounding variety of the region's landscape. Its lower reaches supply water to the San Joaquin Valley, one of California's major agricultural areas.

View of the beach, just north of Westport. Highway 1, which winds along the Pacific Ocean, offers magnificent views of the California coast.

By comparison with trade, mainly in imported goods such as food, clothing and tools from the eastern states of the Union, industry and agriculture were slow to develop. Speculation in commodities, mining and land, and subsequently in stocks and shares, soon proved to be a safer form of gambling than the search for gold which was always a risky business. However, it was not the gambling instinct itself which drew most of the new immigrants to California, but the simple desire of securing a better, happier life by carving out a piece of this earthly paradise for themselves.

Hence, although the California myth was partly fashioned by the irresistible lure of gold, its main roots lie in the general pioneering spirit, the acceptance of risks and uncertainty as everyday facts of life, which led so many Americans to migrate westwards in search of betterment. In the earthly paradise at the edge of the continent, a new set of attitudes emerged which took on the character of a semi-religious creed, allowing maximum scope to the individual in terms of behaviour, the limit being injury to others.

Gold, in the actual physical shape of the proverbially glistening precious metal, was not strictly essential to the California myth, but the memory of the Gold Rush has helped to sustain the legend: the California imagination has transformed the gold deposits into a glittering fictional image of the Golden Fleece, waiting to be discovered by the Argonauts. However, it is on other things that the myth is really founded: on the plentiful natural resources of the region, on its fertile soil and favourable climate, and on the degree of personal freedom which California offers. Nevertheless, there are limits to everything, and people eventually accepted that even the giant redwoods in the Californian forests do not actually grow up to the sky.

Finally, the notion of California as an earthly paradise is additionally sustained by the constant stream of new immigrants, whose grinding poverty leads them to see even the most modest forms of prosperity as visions of utopia. No matter where or how they live, whether enveloped in fabulous luxury or surrounded by the beauties of nature, in the thick of technological progress or in the quiet, secluded world of faded dreams, Californians are always able to find the reality which is the fabric of myth.

A New Reality

It is often the case that reality stubbornly refuses to accommodate itself to the patterns of mythology. The California myth is different: it appears to be verified, rather than unfounded, by the exceptional character of the region, whose giant trees do not actually grow all the way to heaven but come quite close to doing so. And although man's spiralling expectations of utopia have latterly taken something of a jolt, the prevalent mood of resignation as the century gradually draws to a close is contradicted by the sheer beauty of the California landscape, which still appears larger-than-life. The human achievements of the past two centuries have only served to heighten the sense of wonderment, even if the natural environment has suffered in the process.

The attempt to live out the myth of California as a promised land has resulted in a number of impressive achievements: large cities, flourishing towns and villages, immensely productive farms, vast factories, widely-recognized universities and, last but not least, an easygoing lifestyle which is the envy of the world. But the California dream also has its negative side: it encourages the dreamers to transform themselves into pure consumers, interested only in the material aspects of the myth. California hosts a hedonistic society in which the glaring contrast between the extremes of wealth and poverty represent a threat to the very life of the community; it sows the seeds of indifference, which has even more destructive consequences for the myth than the oppression of minorities had in the past. While the rich wallow in excess, others go hungry, and the impoverishment of intellectual life proceeds apace. The poor are encouraged to believe in the manufactured illusions of television and the cinema, and to carry on chasing after the California myth, which has so far eluded them in their everyday lives, by consuming ever-greater quantities of material things. The result is that California, like the country in general, has begun to tread a path leading ultimately to the restriction of individual liberty; thus the people of the state run the risk of forfeiting a part of their guiding myth, and with it, a facet of California's unique character.

However, this dilemma is also opening up new sources of energy which may help to revive the California myth, provided that more people wake up to the problem and realize that even this region, with its seemingly boundless wealth of natural resources, cannot meet the ever-growing material demands of its population. Hence it is necessary to seek political solutions which respect the personal freedom and human dignity of all Californians, taking into account both the need to preserve the natural environment and the fact that there are millions of people who have never even glimpsed the true meaning of the California myth.

*Avenue of the
ants alongside
of Eel River in
the Humboldt
Redwoods State
Park. The giant
redwoods -
also known as
sequoias - are
among the
ld's oldest and
largest trees.*

In Ferndale, southwest of Eureka, splen[did] and plentiful examples of th[e] American vers[ion] of Victorian domestic architecture have been impressively u[ell] preserved . . .

The elementary importance of water illustrates the prevailing state of affairs in a region where even a limited quantity of water makes it possible to open up land for development and to raise agricultural production. Especially in southern California, which houses sixty percent of the state's population but controls only two percent of the water supply, land speculators are increasingly recruiting the services of politicians in order to get their hands on water which is brought via aqueducts and canals from other parts of the region. However, the resulting conflicts have also caused some people to reconsider the significance of water and not only in economic terms.

There are several well-known examples of California success stories which clearly indicate an awareness of these natural limitations. The major landowner on whose property the first gold nuggets were found eventually died in poverty, alone and uncared-for. There was the financier, a ruthless businessman but a generous patron of the arts, who drowned in San Francisco Bay where he had often swum before, and there is also the story of the flamboyant pilot and movie mogul who lived the latter part of his life as a recluse. The limits which these men were ultimately unable to overstep may serve to illustrate the problems of California society as a whole. Hopes and dreams have been nurtured by the fantastic visions of eternal youth, boundless prosperity and unlimited progress.

This situation, with its steadily increasing importance for society, calls for the development and application of a new concept of humanity which will be of universal benefit, since it will extend beyond mankind itself to include other species, together with the elements, earth, air and water, making up our natural environment. From this, the obligation follows to devise a new, ecologically-orientated way of life, which is only possible on the basis of mutual understanding and which must use the limited resources of the region in such a way that its fruits can be enjoyed by all Californians. This new reality places certain restrictions on the California myth, but at the same time it opens up new dimensions in human relationships which in the past have often been distorted by selfishness. There are limits to the accretion of material wealth, but it may be possible to discover riches of another kind. And this, in turn, might help to preserve the world's faith in the notion of California as an earthly and obtainable paradise.

. . . among the
er living docu-
ents of the past
Ferndale is the
den Gait Mer-
cantile, where
sitors can shop
i an authentic
nineteenth-
ntury pioneer
atmosphere.

BEYOND PARADISE
Descriptions and Accounts of California

California, the land of sunshine, fortune, stardom and happiness. In short, the paradigm of utopia itself. These are just some of the glowing images California has created of itself, perpetuated with ardent enterprise and vehemently protected from any loss of sparkle. In our selection of texts, some of the favourite California myths are stripped of this well-polished coat of gloss, such as the Gold Rush, synonymous with California, as well as the great myth-making machine itself, Hollywood. It is the ubiquitous illusion of success and glamour that so often overshadows the natural beauty of this country, a beauty which is beyond the capacity of human creativity.

The Gold Rush

Although chemists and apothecaries have another sign for gold, the popular symbol is 1849. In that year Argonauts from the ends of the earth converged on California and engaged in an orgy of gold gathering that ranks as the greatest of all mining rushes. It all began in an accident, early in 1848, at a sawmill on the south fork of the American River. As that year opened, California did not impress as a land for which great things were in store. Its political future was clouded, its economic prospects strictly limited, its population small, miscellaneous, and discordant.

Yet in the metal that underlay the Sierra foothills and lined the mountain stream beds a force lay dormant that would bring the sleepy province

27

suddenly to life. ... How to get to California? For those whom the gold fever claimed, that was the question. Argonauts in England and Europe would have to go halfway round the world to get to the land of gold. Those in the States, in the winter of '48–'49, faced as difficult a problem.

Geography and history, nevertheless, offered several answers. Beginning in the 1790's, Boston fur ships, China-bound, had rounded Cape Horn or threaded the passage of the Strait of Magellan on a long sea route that passed through California waters. Since the 'twenties, whalers and hide traders and ships of the navy had plied this same course. The Atlantic seaboard – New England and New York, in particular – thus had equipment and know-how for sailing to California. The catch was that on this track of 17,000 or 18,000 miles voyages ran five or six or eight months. What assurance was there that the California gold would last that long?

Another option was to go overland. Jedediah Smith had blazed such a trail in 1826. Other intrepid beaver trappers followed and in the 'forties their paths were widened by pioneer settlers in covered wagons, by government agents such as Frémont, and by the marching soldiers of the Army of the West.

Here also was a catch. The overland trails were not reckoned open for travel until April or May, which would not land one in the diggings until August or September. Again rose the question, would all the gold be gone?

The third main pathway of the gold rush – the broken-voyage route, with a land crossing at Panama, Nicaragua, or Mexico – had not been so popular before 1848. Yet the two official dispatch bearers had traveled this way, Beale by Mexico and Loeser by Panama. Some Argonauts may also have remembered that, on the eve of the war, when President Polk wanted an urgent message delivered to California, courier Archibald Gillespie went by Vera Cruz, Mexico City, Mazatlán, and Hawaii.

Furthermore, the Panama route had two great advantages over its competitors. It was an all-year route. Over it one could start for California immediately and hope to arrive in a matter of weeks, in plenty of time to get to the mines as the season of '49 opened. And, best of all, the Panama route boasted public transportation; one could engage passage on the steamers of the United States Mail Steamship Company and the Pacific Mail. ...

The irreverent, it must be admitted, sometimes ask whether the gold of California did not do more harm than good. Anyone who follows the boulder-strewn trail of the dredger, visits the gaping holes and barren debris piles of the hydraulickers, and contemplates the unsightly dumps of the hard-rock mines will be conscious of some of the damage done. Add then the muddying of the streams that made the salmon stop running, the silting of the lower rivers that slowed and then stopped the river boats, the devastation of farm lands by floodwaters and tailings.

The Indians of the Sierra foothills were early victims, first in having their sources of food supply laid waste and then in the "wars" of extermination. Marshall got no profit from the discovery and Sutter lost his all. On the sea routes, shipwreck, cholera, and Panama fever claimed victims; on the overland routes, cholera, mountain fever, traffic accidents, and Indian attacks. In the mines, mishaps and illness afflicted the gold seekers, and another untold number went to their graves. The gold rush, it must be admitted, was responsible for more bereavements, more broken homes, that the War with Mexico.

The historian JOHN WALTON CAUGHY has written a number of books on California. As well as tracing the history of the Gold Rush, he also examines its repercussions for the country and its people.

The San Francisco Earthquake

It was one which was long called the "great" earthquake, and is doubtless so distinguished till this day. It was just after noon, on a bright October day. I was coming down Third Street. The only objects in motion anywhere in sight in that thickly built and populous quarter were a man in a buggy behind me, and a street car wending slowly up the cross street. Otherwise, all was solitude and a Sabbath stillness. As I turned the corner, around a frame house, there was a great rattle and jar, and it occurred to me that here was an item! – no doubt a fight in that house. Before I could turn and seek the door, there came a really terrific shock; the ground seemed to roll under me in waves, interrupted by a violent joggling up and down, and there was a heavy grinding noise as of brick houses rubbing together. I fell up against the frame house and hurt my elbow. I knew what it was, now, and from mere reportorial instinct, nothing else, took out my watch and noted the time of day; at that moment a third and still severer shock came, and as I reeled about on the pavement trying to keep my footing, I saw a sight! The entire front of a tall four-storey brick building in Third Street sprang outward like a door and fell sprawling across the street, raising a dust like a great volume of smoke! And here came the buggy – overboard went the man, and in less time than I can tell it the vehicle was distributed in small

Ferndale has successfully preserved its idyllic old-world character: town contains almost nothing that rings even faintly of modernity.

Near Monterey. The fields of California are like a kaleidoscope whose colours change with the seasons.

fragments along three hundred yards of street. One could have fancied that somebody had fired a charge of chair-rounds and rags down the thoroughfare. The street car had stopped, the horses were rearing and plunging, the passengers were pouring out at both ends, and one fat man had crashed half-way through a glass window on one side of the car, got wedged fast, and was squirming and screaming like an impaled madman. Every door of every house, as far as the eye could reach, was vomiting a stream of human beings; and almost before one could execute a wink and begin another, there was a massed multitude of people stretching in endless procession down every street my position commanded. Never was solemn solitude turned into teeming life quicker.

Of the wonders wrought by "the great earthquake," these were all that came under my eye; but the tricks it did elsewhere, and far and wide over the town, made toothsome gossip for nine days. The destruction of property was trifling – the injury to it was wide-spread and somewhat serious.

The "curiosities" of the earthquake were simply endless. Gentlemen and ladies who were sick, or were taking a siesta, or had dissipated till a late hour and were making up lost sleep, thronged into the public streets in all sorts of queer apparel, and some without any at all. One woman who had been washing a naked child, ran down the street holding it by the ankles as if it were a dressed turkey. Prominent citizens who were supposed to keep the Sabbath strictly, rushed out of saloons in their shirt-sleeves, with billiard cues in their hands. Dozens of men, with necks swathed in napkins, rushed from barbers' shops, lathered to the eyes or with one cheek clean shaved and the other still bearing a hairy stubble. Horses broke from stables, and a frightened dog rushed up a short attic ladder and out on to a roof, and when his scare was over had not the nerve to go down again the same way he had gone up. A prominent editor flew downstairs, in the principal hotel, with nothing on but one brief under-garment – met a chambermaid, and exclaimed:

"Oh, what *shall* I do? Where shall I go?"

She responded with naive serenity:

"If you have no choice, you might try a clothing store!"

A certain foreign consul's lady was the acknowledged leader of fashion, and every time she appeared in anything new or extraordinary, the ladies in the vicinity made a raid on their husbands' purses and arrayed themselves similarly. One man who had suffered considerably and growled accordingly, was standing at the window when the shocks came, and the next instant the consul's wife, just out of the bath, fled by with no other apology for clothing than – a bath towel! The sufferer rose superior to the terrors of the earthquake, and said to his wife:

"Now *that* is something I *like!* Get out your towel, my dear!"

The plastering that fell from ceilings in San Francisco that day would have covered several acres of ground. For some days afterward, groups of eyeing and pointing men stood about many a bulilding, looking at long zigzag cracks that extended from the eaves to the ground. Four feet of the tops of three chimneys on one house were broken square off and turned around in such a way as to completely stop the draught. A crack a hundred feet long gaped open six inches wide in the middle of one street, and then shut together again with such force as to ridge up the meeting earth like a slender grave. A lady, sitting in her rocking and quaking parlour, saw the wall part at the ceiling, open and shut twice, like a mouth, and then drop the end of a brick on the floor like a tooth. She was a woman easily disgusted with foolishness, and she arose and went out of there. One lady who was coming downstairs was astonished to see a bronze Hercules lean forward on its pedestal as if to strike her with its club. They both reached the bottom of the flight at the same time, – the woman insensible from the fright. Her child, born some little time afterwards, was club-footed. However – on second thought – if the reader see any coincidence in this, he must do it at his own risk.

The first shock brought down two or three huge organ-pipes in one of the churches. The minister, with uplifted hands, was just closing the services. He glanced up, hesitated, and said:

"However, we will omit the benediction!" – and the next instant there was a vacany in the atmosphere where he had stood.

After the first shock, an Oakland minister said:

"Keep your seats! There is no better place to die than this" – And added, after the third:

"But outside is good enough!" He then skipped out at the back door.

Such another destruction of mantel ornaments and toilet bottles as the earthquake created, San Francisco never saw before. There was hardly a girl or a matron in the city but suffered loses of this kind. Suspended pictures were thrown down, but oftener still, by a curious freak of the earthquake's humour, they were whirled completely around with their faces to the wall! There was great difference of opinion, at first, as to the course or direction the earthquake travelled, but water that splashed out of various tanks and

A gold-diggers' wooden chapel in the Bodie State Historic Park. During the Gold Rush, Bodie was a thriving town with some 10,000 residents but it fell into decay when the gold ran out. The reconstructed miners' settlement conveys something of the heady atmosphere which reigned in California after the first gold nuggets were discovered on the American River in 1848.

buckets settled that. Thousands of people were made so sea-sick by the rolling and pitching of floors and streets that they were weak and bedridden for hours, and some few for even days, afterward. Hardly an individual escaped nausea entirely.

The queer earthquake episodes that formed the staple of San Francisco gossip for the next week would fill a much larger book than this, and so I will diverge from the subject.

MARK TWAIN (1835-1910) is regarded as one of America's most famous writers. As well as his novels depicting life in the South, he wrote numerous books about his travels. This excerpt is taken from his 1906 work, "The Innocents at Home".

Concerning Hollywood . . .

Obviously there are three ways of looking at Hollywood: one as an outsider familiar only with the fringe; one as a worker in the heart of the whole thing; and the third is in detached retrospect. Fortunately, during my twenty years, I have looked in all three ways. The result is I do not laugh at Hollywood.

I like a lot of the people there. Frequently I like to go around with them for an evening or two. They can be as much fun as a boatload of irresponsible kids. But also, in a sharpshooting way, they are so much smarter than most of us that it is better not to take seriously their flattery or their promises or to allow one's own reception to be taken too much to heart. Today with them is a different day, and yesterday was another, and tomorrow is 'way off in the distance somewhere. Their type of business is such that each person, of necessity, must think of himself first. This is essential for each individual's survival, nor should he or she be blamed for it. They are not farmers.

Nor, fundamentally, do the Hollywood workers (the directors, the actors, the writers, the producers) ever really have a good time. So much is at stake that they constantly are worried, even at play. And they work constantly, even when at play. They constantly are trying to put jigsaw pieces together, to make them match, for their own betterment, for their own next job.

Few of them, despite what they say, can ever really get used to the phraseology of such big money. Their previous backgrounds have not allowed them to swing into the surprise riches gracefully. Nor are the actual riches as rich as the figures promise. Too much has to be taken out of each check before they can see

any of the money; government taxes, state taxes, agents' fees, managers' fees, labor pensions and se-curity fees – with all of these automatically subtracted from each check, the left-over often is far less than half the original. Sometimes only a quarter.

And this is the left-over which must buy clothes, must pay the hair-dressers, must meet the rents, must settle the entertainmet bills, must be spectacularly generous to all charities, and finally must keep all the dependents.

I have gone through the experiment, in company with Hollywood people, of trying to have a good time in Hollywood. They are, naturally, as desperate for happiness as anybody else. They are more desperate, actually, and for this reason try harder. I am speaking in generalities now, but in this instance the general-ities cover at least ninety per cent of those who have big jobs. Unaccustomed to moderation in anything, they reach for the extremes, as if by mere mass pres-sure they can force happiness to come their way. When they gamble they gamble bigger and harder and longer. When they play the races they really play them. When they have a big party it is a big party. Yet here is the catch: I have seen some of them, when down at my home on the ocean, literally beam with

ecstasy over what to me is the commonplace, the moon over a quiet sea and a simple bonfire to cook my meal.

Like so many writers who spent time in Hollywood, MAX MILLER wrote about his personal experience. His views behind the scenes reveal the efforts involved in achieving and maintaining the success and fame Hollywood promises.

... and Chinatown

Chinatown, even in the smaller towns, was always picturesque, always of interest to the newcomer. I don't know how it was managed, but a Chinaman could, with a varnished duck, a few yards of dizzy muslin, and some red paper, throw glamour about the most commonplace old frame building. But the Chinatown of San Francisco was famed. An incred-ible number of these people were crowded into a space four blocks square. In sight, sound, and smell it was a miniature replica of a Chinese city. It was one of the sights for "tourii." By daytime they wandered through it in droves. By night small, select, and shud-dery parties got themselves a "detective" by way of protection, and were led into awesome places, culminating in gambling hells and opium dens and cellars that went down three or four stories underground – we counted the flights of stairs! They departed, firmly convinced that they knew all about China and the Chinese. They had seen nothing – they could see nothing without credentials – of the beautiful upper-story homes and charming family life of the great merchants, or even the sober social clubs, where, beneath portraits of the president and the Emperor, men sat quietly a ebony-wood tables shuffling the mah-jongg tiles.

Incidentally, these alleged underground works were amusing. The illusion was perfect – for it was an illusion. You entered from the street; you went down a flight of steps into an cellar full of smoke and gamblers; you went down another flight of steps into a subcellar full of smoke and opium fiends; you went down another flight of steps into a subsubcellar full of smoke and sinister hatchet men; and so on, if your "detective" was a good thrill picker and had the proper connections; until, with a shudder of ecstasy, you realized you were four, five stories deep in the bowels of the earth – with, probably, secret passages extending in all directions! You climbed back up all those stairs and wrote postal cards on which you used the phrase "a veritable rabbit warren." Two facts escaped your notice – that, invariably, you made these subterranean visits at night, and that even in the lowest story the air was passably breathable.

The explanation is simple. San Francisco's Chinatown is built on a steep side hill. The story which is the third or fourth when viewed from the downhill side of a building becomes the ground floor when entered from the street above. After dark this fact is not apparent. All the "detective" has to do is to take his "tourii" in at the upper street level. From that nethermost "four stories underground" he could have let them out directly on the level of the alleyway below, but that would never have done. It was a neat trick, loyally sustained by true Californians. The fire and earthquake of 1906 were supposed to have filled all these underground works, and the modern guides to the modern Chinatown have not dared revive the hoax.

Modern Chinatown is well worth a visit, but it is in no sense the old. It is more consciously picturesque. Many of its new buildings, erected after the fire, are deliberately of Chinese architecture, with curving roofs and red and gold decorations. There is better display of goods, better English spoken. Things are more in order. My collection contains little of it. It is much more sanitary and businesslike and like all the rest, I admit. So I presume are the modern alert and snappy young Chinamen I see on the streets. But I know little of them. At the Bohemian Club, shrewd, wrinkled, lively little old Fong used to stand behind his own especial little counter. Heaven alone knew the tally of his years. Only the very oldest members knew the period of his service. For some time before he retired its daily duration was but two hours – from four o'clock to six. He served tea to those who wanted it and cackled hilariously to those members he considered his especial friends. Each Thursday the club gives some informal entertainment under direction of a member designated as Sire for the evening. A few years ago Fong announced, "I give pa'ty," and he did – to the whole membership able to attend. "Fong Night," it was called, and there were Chinese food and Chinese music and souvenirs for everybody, and there was a notable gathering to do him honor. And through him, I think, to his beloved vanishing race.

STEWART EDWARD WHITE has written both fiction and non-fiction books on California. His portrayal of San Francisco's Chinatown before the fire and earthquake in 1906 is taken from his "My Ming Collection", first published in 1921.

Through Death Valley

On leaving Lone Pine the desert began again, miles of desert, and suddenly, on the shores of a half dried-up lake, a handful of wooden shacks; salt is extracted from these dead waters, pyramids of white crystals shine in the sun. There was not a blade of grass and, at ten o'clock in the morning, not a puff of wind; railway lines take half-rusted wagons to Lone Pine, but there is no train near; and it is not at all true, as a kindly legend has it, that every American workman has a car; those around here are without them. They are crushed between the implacable sky and the mummified earth. Heat, salt and boredom: this place, so picturesque to drive through, must be an inferno.

After this we would not see another house for a long time. The road curled through mountains where ochre mingled with crude violet. We came to the first valley, deep between walls of rock; dry, bluish grass covered the bottom slashed by a road: straight and headstrong the road cut through the depression, then climbed in spirals to the crest ahead; in this place, hostile to men, it is a touching declaration of man's work, for it is the road which gives significance to a country that was for long a dangerous pass; all the tragic migrations of the pioneers come to life on this stiff white ribbon. Many adventurers, ploughing their way on foot towards California, hoped to cut short

e cholla cactus
one of the rare
ms of plant life
which can be
n at the Joshua
Tree National
Monument, a
large nature
serve in south-
rn California.
possible to tell
the age of a
cactus by
counting the
cylindrical
shoots, like the
rings of a
tree trunk.

Mann's Chinese Theater, Hollywood Boulevard's most famous cinema, has a giant auditorium whose walls are lined with silk.

their journey by avoiding the high crests and by cutting their way through Death Valley and Panamint Valley. Many of them perished in these salty deserts where water was seldom found and the heat was unbearable. To-day at the entrance to Death Valley there is a police post, and travellers have to write their names in a register; they are advised not to wander from the highroad, for, above all in summer, to get lost or have an puncture on the side roads may prove fatal.

It is not long since Scott, the old hero of Death Valley, whose "country house" is still shown, was riding through the depression when he met an old couple whose car had refused to go on. He gave them a little water and promised to bring help; but in the time it would take him to go and come back, the unfortunate couple would die of thirst and sunstroke. Scott thought for a moment, pulled out his revolver and shot them. His house rises up amid the sand dunes that for miles recall the Sahara. We passed it on our left and drove over stony ground and rimed salt: the huge depression is merely an ancient lake that the sun has drunk dry. Already at this time of the year the heat is overpowering, we were in a muck-sweat. In two hours time we reached a place called

"The Furnace", which the emigrants looked upon as the heart of Hades. It is a tiny oasis with a few springs and some weakly trees; in the last century when the springs dried up, the emigrants could do nothing more than wait for death, but to-day they have arranged things so that there is always water. There is a luxurious hotel with a terrace, where people sprawling in deck-chairs take sunbaths, and a "court" on a more modest scale, made up of cabins grouped round a cafeteria.

We lunched, then went to see old relics exhibited on a kind of esplanade: the trekkers' carts with their green tarpaulins; the apparatus which served to extract and purify the gold; the little wagons used to transport the borate once the mines were worked out. (In those days they did fifteen miles a day with difficulty.) Here were the first public buses – old carts which carry the inscription in big letters: "Death Valley Stage". Those epic times never seemed so unreal as here where they really happened. I felt the great heat of the sun, saw the heights, measured the immensity of the distances: how could one believe that whole families had crossed these barren lands without even the help of a road? Some waited here for months for the more robust members of the

. . . the California world is full of colour. Here, a vision of the Stars and Stripes and America's youth in front of the Transamerica Building.

caravan, who had gone ahead, to return and rescue them, and they were saved and tasted of the fruits of California. Was it possible that this had really happened, and scarcely a hundred years ago? Never before and nowhere else had I felt the excitement so strongly which springs from the past of the Far West.

The French feminist, philosopher and novelist SIMONE DE BEAUVOIR visited California as part of her nation-wide lecture tour in 1947. The wonderment of Death Valley is mixed with De Beauvoir's own sense of bewilderment at the achievements of those who crossed this stretch of desert over one hundred years previous.

In Protest

Proclamation to the Great White Father ... 1969

We, the native Americans, re-claim the land known as Alcatraz Island in the name of all American Indians by right of discovery.

We wish to be fair and honorable in our dealings with the Caucasian inhabitants of this land, and hereby offer the following treaty:

We will purchase said Alcatraz Island for twenty-four dollars (24) in glass beads and red cloth, a prece-dent set by the white man's purchase of a similar island about 300 years ago. We know that $ 24 in trade goods for these 16 acres is more than was paid when Manhattan Island was sold, but we know that land values have risen over the years. Our offer of $1.24 per acre is greater than the 47¢ per acre the white men are now paying the California Indians for their land.

We will give to the inhabitants of this island a portion of the land for their own to be held in trust by the American Indian Affairs and by the bureau of Caucasian Affairs to hold in perpetuity – for as long as the sun shall rise and the rivers go down to the sea.

We will further guide the inhabitants in the proper way of living.

We will offer them our religion, our education, our life-ways, in order to help them achieve our level of civilization and thus raise them and all their white brothers up from their savage and unhappy state.

We offer this treaty in good faith and wish to be fair and honorable in our dealings with all white men.

We feel that this so-called Alcatraz Island is more than suitable for an Indian Reservation, as deter-mined by the white man's own standards. By this we mean that this place resembles most Indian reservations in that:

1. It is isolated from modern facilities, and without adequate means of transportation.
2. It has no fresh running water.
3. It has inadequate sanitation facilities.
4. There are no oil or mineral rights.
5. There is no industry and so unemployment is very great.
6. There are no health care facilities.
7. The soil is rocky and non-productive; and the land does not support game.
8. There are no educational facilities.
9. The population has always exceeded the land base.
10. The population has always been held as prisoners and kept dependent upon others.

Further, it would be fitting and symbolic that ships from all over the world, entering the Golden Gate, would first see Indian land, and thus be reminded of the true history of this nation. This tiny island would be a symbol of the great lands once ruled by free and noble Indians.

In 1969 a group of Indians occupied Alcatraz Island in San Francisco Bay. Calling themselves "Indians of All Tribes", they claimed the right of possession of the island under a Sioux treaty of 1868.

The Missions

There have been few visitors to Southern California who have not made a tour of the Missions, purchased a postcard with a picture of Ramona's birthplace, and attended a performance of the Mission Play. With a boldness more comic than brazen, the synthetic past has been kept alive by innumerable pageants, fiestas, and outdoor enactments of one kind or another, by the restoration of the Missions; and by the establishment of such curious spectacles as Olvera Street in the Old Plaza sections of Los Angeles.

The symbols of this synthetic past are three in number: the Franciscan padre praying at sundown in the Mission garden, lovely Ramona and brave Alessandro fleeing through the foothills of Mt. San Jacinto, and the Old Spanish Don sunning himself in the courtyard of his rancho. Around these sacred symbols, the legends have grown. According to the authorized version, the officially approved script, the Indians were devoted to the Franciscans, and, with the collapse of the Mission system, lost their true friends and devoted defenders. ... The other side of

the legend has to do with the idyllic period "before the gringos" came, when the Spanish residents of Alta California, all members of one big happy guitar-twanging family, danced the fandango and lived out days of beautiful indolence in lands of the sun that expand the soul. ... Indian furnished the labor power for the far-flung Mission enterprises. They cleared the ground, planted the first vineyards, constructed the irrigation ditches and canals, and built the Missions. The Indian influence explains the singular dichotomy in the cultural traditions of the region between what is termed "Spanish," and is therefore valuable and praiseworthy, and what is termed "Mexican" and is therefore undesirable. For while Indian and Spanish are, in a sense, oppositional terms in this cultural tradition, the Indian and Mexican influences tend to merge.

Somehow this Indian background got lost in the transition from Spanish to English. There was much lore and information about the Indians in the Spanish archives which did not reappear in English until long after most of the Indians had been exterminated. Even after the Spanish chronicles began to appear in English, the record remained incomplete and misleading.

When the great commercial value of the Mission tradition was discovered around 1888 – an event of major importance in the cultural history of Southern California – the healthy realism of such California historians as Bancroft, Forbes, and Hittell was largely forgotten and the Franciscan version of the Indian was accepted at face value. In a region of rapid social change, such as Southern California, traditions have a tendency to become lost, distorted, or confused, with part of the confusion being for poseful and part fortuitous. It is not surprising, therefore, that a bizarre pattern of cultural miscegenation should have developed in the region in which the Indian influence was almost wholly obscured.

Thus, to this day, the word "Indian" in Southern California has its sacred and profance connotations. In the flesh – in the areas where they still survive – Indians remain "Digger Indians," fabled in local folklore for their thievery, filth, and lechery. But, with each annual production of the Ramona Pageant, pictures of godlike Indians in battle-dress appear in the rotogravure sections of the Los Angeles *Times* and the Indian Love Call echoes throughout Southern California.

In her examination of California's falsified historical and cultural icons, CAREY MCWILLIAMS discusses the missions of Southern California and their relationship to the native Indian life-style.

The historic Hotel Del Coronado near San Diego, a late Victorian folly which has had its fair share of scandals involving stars and starlets.

The notorious smog of Los Angeles often plays strange tricks with the light, blurring the distinction between reality and the world of make-believe.

The Valley of the Sacramento

We were now in the valley of plenty. Our poor teeth, which had been laboring on the filelike consistency of pilot bread, had now a respite, in the agreeable task of masticating from the 'flesh pots' of California.

As we determined to lay over during the day, our wagon master, Traverse, concluded to butcher an ox, and the hungry Arabs of our train were regaled with a feast of dead kine. Feeling an aristocratic longing for a rich beef steak, I determined to have one. There was not a particle of fat in the steak to make gravy, nor was there a slice of bacon to be had to fry it with, and the flesh was as dry and as hard as a bone.

But a nice broiled steak, with a plenty of gravy, I would have – and I had it. The inventive genius of an emigrant is almost constantly called forth on the plains, and so in my case, I laid a nice cut on the coals, which, instead of broiling, only burnt and carbonized like a piece of wood, and when one side was turned to cinder, I whopped it over to make charcoal of the other.

To make butter gravy, I melted a stearin candle, which I poured over the delicious tit-bit, and, smacking my lips, sat down to my feast, the envy of several lookers on. I sopped the first mouthful in the nice looking gravy, and put it between my teeth, when the gravy cooled almost instantly, and the roof of my mouth and my teeth were coated all over with a covering like hard beeswax, making mastication next to impossible. 'How does it go?' asked one.

'O, first rate,' said I, struggling to get a hard, dry morsel down my throat; and cutting another piece, which was free from the delicious gravy, 'Come, try it,' said I; 'I have more than I can eat (which was true). You are welcome to it.'

The envious, hungry soul sat down and, putting a large piece between his teeth, after rolling it about in his mouth awhile, deliberately spit it out, saying, with an oath, that 'Chips and beeswax are hard fare, even for a starving man.'

Ah, how hard words and want of sentiment will steal over one's better nature on the plains.

As for the rest of the steak, we left it to choke the wolves.

ALONZO DELANO was advised that a journey across the plains would benefit his health. He set off from Missouri for California in 1849. It was the height of the Gold Rush and Delano intended to make his fortune selling goods to the miners.

The beach at Big Sur on Highway 1, one of the world's most beautiful roads which runs for one hundred miles/one hundred-sixty o-metres along the unspoiled coastline of the Pacific Ocean.

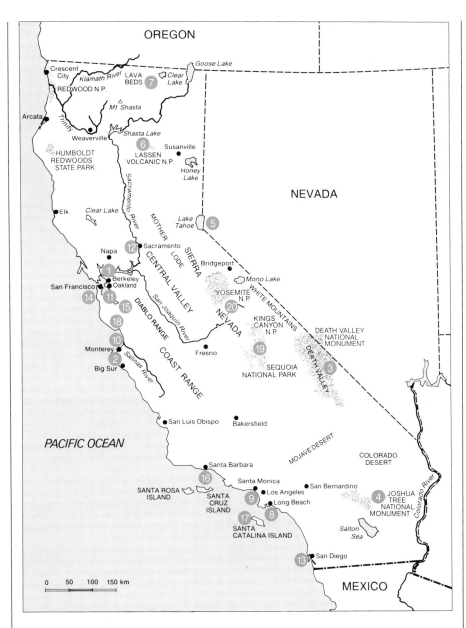

perature may be so high that shorts and short-sleeved cotton shirts are the order of the day. In the winter, rain is frequent, with heavy snowfalls in the mountains, whereas the summer is generally dry. However, exceptions to the rule are always possible, and before travelling anywhere in California, it is advisable to enquire about the prevailing weather conditions at your destination.

INFORMATION

Enquiries may be addressed to the California Office of Tourism, which has two branches, one in Sacramento (1121 L St., Suite 103, Sacramento, CA, USA, 95814, tel.: 916-322-1397) and the other near Los Angeles (PO Box 9278, T98, Dept. 1003, Van Nuys, CA, USA, 91409, tel.: 800-862-2543).

Information about the state parks may be obtained from the California State Park System, Department of Parks and Recreation, PO Box 942896, Sacramento, CA, USA, 94296, tel.: 916-445-6477. For details concerning the national parks, contact the National Park Service, Fort Mason, Bldg. 201, Bay and Franklin Streets, San Francisco, CA, USA, 94123, tel.: 415-556-0560.

For passport and visa regulations, consult the United States Embassy or consulate in your home country.

TRANSPORT

The best way of travelling around California is by car, but take care to avoid the rush hour in and around the main cities: from 7 to 9 a.m. and 4 to 6 p.m., traffic conditions tend to be chaotic. It is advisable to book a hire car in advance and pick it up at the airport when you arrive. Most of the major car-hire companies have offices at the main airports.

In some cases, tolls are levied for travellers on bridges and roads. Steep mountain roads are closed to caravans. Additional supplies of oil and water should be carried when travelling long distances in the desert. Ensure that you have a reliable road map and study it carefully before setting out: it will give you all the information you need to plan your journey.

Forecasting the weather in the desert and mountains is strictly for greenhorns:

GENERAL INFORMATION

SIZE AND LOCATION. With an area of 158,693 square miles (411,014 square kilometres), California is the third largest state in the United States. The southernmost of the three Pacific states, it lies between the 32nd and 42nd parallels. It is bordered to the east by Nevada and Arizona, to the north by Oregon and to the south by Mexico. The highest and lowest points of the region are Mount Whitney and Death Valley, respectively 14,495 feet (4,418 metres) above and 282 feet (86 metres) below sea level. Death Valley is the lowest point in the entire country.

Local time is Pacific Standard Time (PST), which is eight hours behind Greenwich Mean Time and nine hours behind Central European Time. This should be taken into account when making overseas phone calls.

CLIMATE. The California climate is generally mild, especially along the sixty mile/one hundred kilometre coastal strip where most of the population lives. Here, the summer heat and winter cold are tempered by the Pacific Ocean, but further inland, the climate is more extreme. The temperature often fluctuates considerably within the same area. Even in summer, the weather in the Bay Area around San Francisco may be cool and misty, making jackets and pullovers essential. However, a mere thirty miles/fifty kilometres inland, the tem-

more experienced travellers know all too well that surprises are the rule rather than the exception. In the desert, sudden torrential rainstorms can cause severe flooding; in the mountain regions, shifts in the weather may bring hail, black ice, snow and avalanches. In order to cut down on unpleasant surprises of this sort, drivers are advised to contact the relevant visitor center and enquire about weather conditions along the route.

The public transport system in California leaves a good deal to be desired. However, given the requisite amount of patience, it is possible to visit a large number of places by skilfully combining various means of public transport, such as Greyhound and Trailway Buses, the local transit systems in the big cities and the Amtrak railway network.

CURRENCY AND TIPPING

Cash is accepted everywhere, but carrying around large wads of banknotes is inadvisable: for transactions of any significant size, use credit cards instead. In California, and in general throughout the United States, tipping is universal since bills rarely include a service charge; hotel staff, waiters and taxi-drivers rely on tips for the better part of their income. As a rule, fifteen percent of the bill is adequate. One dollar per piece of luggage is the going rate for hotel porters carrying your bags to your room; chambermaids expect a tip of up to two dollars per room per night.

SIGHTSEEING

California abounds in remains of the various Indian cultures. These fascinating documents of the past can be seen in the national and state parks, Indian cultural centres, and museums of anthropology. The largest Indian reservation is at Hoopa Valley in the northwest region of the state, home of the Hupa and Yoruk tribes. The Indians are understandably sensitive about the treatment meted out to them in the past by the white population, and insist on their privacy being respected. Consequently, if you plan to visit an Indian reservation, it is essential to enquire in advance whether sightseers are welcome.

Most of the documents of California's history are from the nineteenth and twentieth centuries. In many cases, the traces of past events are immediately visible: the history of the state appears to come alive before the visitors' eyes, and it is this sense of immediacy which makes the buildings and artifacts interesting, despite their relatively recent vintage. The monuments of natural history are a quite different matter, since their fascination lies precisely in their antiquity. Nevertheless, whether looking at the glacial striations on the steep granite walls of a canyon, or the petrified torrent of lava at the base of an extinct volcano, one can trace the history of an entire geological epoch, set out with a vividness as if the events had happened only yesterday. The only thing detracting from the enjoyment of California's beauties is the presence of large crowds of other people with the same intention. Just as when visiting the Tower of London, the Uffizi Gallery in Florence or the castles of Bavaria at the height of the holiday season, it is helpful in California to regard one's fellow-tourists as part of the spectacle. (They, of course, are "tourists", whereas we are "visitors".)

Most of the parks, museums, amusement centres and other attractions charge an entrance fee.

POINTS OF INTEREST

Circled numbers refer to the map on page 48; italicized numbers refer to the colour photographs.

The following abbreviations are used in the route suggestions: I = interstate, US = US highway, S = state highway. As on most maps and road signs in California, distances and altitudes are given in miles and feet.

ANAHEIM. Situated in Orange County south of Los Angeles, Anaheim (pop. 273,500) is the world's capital of family entertainment. *Disneyland* (1313 Harbor Boulevard, on the I 5 from Los Angeles) is a fantasy paradise exciting visitors by its sheer variety. It is divided into several theme areas including "Main Street USA", "Adventureland", "Bear Country", "Fantasyland" and "Tomorrowland".

Opening hours vary considerably. Generally speaking, Disneyland is open daily from 9 a.m. to midnight (Saturdays to 1 a.m.) in the summer months; at other times of the year, it is open most days of the week between 10 a.m. and 6 p.m., with the extended hours of 9 a.m. to midnight on Saturdays and public holidays. To avoid disappointments visitors are advised to call the information service (tel.: 714-999-4565) in advance.

BERKELEY ①**.** It is often said that Berkeley, on the east side of the San Francisco Bay, is not so much a city as a state of mind. The *University of California at Berkeley*, founded in 1868, is the oldest of the nine campuses comprising the University of California. One of the country's leading educational institutions, it is a hive of intellectual activity, continually studying the many and various problems of American society. The campus is magnificently sited in the area bounded by Hearst Avenue and Bancroft Way, to the east of Oxford Street. Guided tours are available (tel.: 415-642-5215). From the Sather Tower, there is a fine view of the university, the city and parts of the bay. Further points of interest include the Botanical Garden, the Lawrence Hall of Science, the Robert H. Lowie Museum of Anthropology and the University Art Museum.

BEVERLY HILLS, an island of elegant, lavishly appointed villas in the seething sprawl of Los Angeles, has numerous film stars among its residents. Driving along Santa Monica Boulevard or walking through the centre of town, one has only a vague impression of the luxury concealed behind the façades. Rodeo Drive is packed with art galleries and jewellers' shops.

BODIE STATE HISTORIC PARK, is a museum with the remains of a mining town, set on a high, bare plateau twenty miles/thirty-two kilometres southeast of Bridgeport (take US 395 and turn off onto S 270). Between 1870 and 1880, the gold mines here were among the most productive in California, and the town had some 10,000 residents who were noted for their lawlessness. Eventually the gold ran out, and mining here finally ceased in the 1950s. *33*

BURBANK. One of the largest cities in the San Fernando Valley, Burbank is noted for its film and television studios. At the NBC studios (300 W. Alameda

Avenue, tel.: 818-840-3537), guided tours are available, giving visitors a chance to take a peek behind the scenes and see how television programmes are made, along with the possibility of taking a screen test or participating in a studio audience during a live taping.

CARMEL ②. Located in the southern part of the Monterey Peninsula, Carmel is a charming coastal town which has gone to considerable lengths to preserve its old-world atmosphere. Apart from the well-tended beach with its long stretch of white sand, the town's main attraction is its exclusive shopping facilities, including boutiques, art galleries and handicraft workshops. The *Mission San Carlos Borromeo del Rio Carmelo*, or Carmel Mission as it generally known, was founded by Father Junípero Serra, a Franciscan missionary who died in the town in 1784. Nearly one hundred years later, in 1882, his tomb in the mission church was rediscovered, together with the burial place of Fermín Francisco de Lasuén, who succeeded Serra as president of the Catholic mission to southern California. *Point Lobos State Reserve*, four miles/six kilometres south of Carmel, is the most impressive nature reserve on the entire California coast. Monterey cypresses and wild flowers abound, while sea-lions bask in the sun on the numerous rocks rearing up out of the sea only a short distance away from the steep cliffs. *46*

COLOMA, on S 49, stands in the foothills of the Sierra Nevadas, about forty-five miles/seventy kilometres northeast of Sacramento. It was here that the Gold Rush began in January 1848, when James W. Marshall, a carpenter from New Jersey, discovered a golden nugget at the site of a sawmill he was building on the American River. The event had far-reaching consequences and accelerated the development of California, formerly a province of Mexico, which, in 1850, became the thirty-first state in the Union. The *Marshall Gold Discovery State Park* features a replica of the sawmill and numerous other souvenirs of the Gold Rush era.

COLUMBIA, near Sonora, just off S 49, was one of the major gold-prospecting sites in the period between 1850 and

The Pacific coast near Carmel.

Golden Canyon in Death Valley.

1870. Although the population dwindled when mining ceased, Columbia never became a ghost town. Some parts of the town centre were preserved in their original state, and others have since been reconstructed. The *Columbia State Historic Park* provides a detailed picture of everyday life in a nineteenth-century mining settlement.

DEATH VALLEY NATIONAL MONUMENT ③. The most popular time to visit Death Valley, one of the hottest places in the world, is between November and April. The landscape is extraordinarily impressive and varied, with deep canyons and high mountains, shimmering sand-dunes and salt-pans on which the harsh sunlight appears to dance. Together with the geological peculiarities of Death Valley, its abundance of rare plants and animals heightens the impression of California's uniqueness, as a region which is geographically isolated from the rest of the United States. In the past, Death Valley was a major centre of borax mining, and near the *Furnace Creek Visitor Center* there is a restored borax works which is open to visitors. The exhibits include several of the huge waggons, used to transport the mineral, pulled by teams of up to twenty mules. *17, 19*

DEVIL'S POSTPILE NATIONAL MONUMENT is a bizarre rock formation standing 7,600 feet/2,316 metres above sea level near the Mammoth Lakes in the eastern part of the Sierra Nevadas. It is located on the S 203 running west from US 395. The wall of symmetrical basalt pillars, approximately sixty feet/eighteen metres high, was formed by the action of

Hollywood Boulevard, Los Angeles.

A fine specimen of the Joshua Tree.

glaciers on solidified lava. Enquiries should be addressed to the Ranger Station, tel.: 619-934-2289.

ESCONDIDO is the site of the *San Diego Wild Animal Park,* five miles/eight kilometres south of I 15 (exit at Rancho Parkway). The animals which roam freely in the extensive grounds of the park include zebras, giraffes, elephants and tigers. Parts of the grounds have been landscaped to replicate the animals' natural habitats in Africa and Asia. A single-line model railway conveys visitors to the individual areas.

FRESNO (pop. 367,700) is the urban centre of the **San Joaquin Valley,** the large irrigated region of California where grapes, figs and cotton are grown in vast quantities. The valley is one of North America's major suppliers of agricultural produce. The origins of California's agrobusiness are documented by exhibits at the *Kearney Mansion Museum* in Kearney Park, seven miles/eleven kilometres west of Fresno, and the *Meux Home Museum* in Tulare.

GLEN ELLEN, on S 12 in Sonoma Valley, is the site of the *Jack London State Historic Park.* Here, visitors can see the

ranch where the writer lived until his suicide in 1916, and the ruins of his home. He is buried on the estate grounds. The museum has an extensive collection of documents and artifacts relating to Jack London's life, especially to the period which he spent roaming the South Seas.

HOLLYWOOD, formerly a town in its own right, was incorporated into Los Angeles in 1910. Although Hollywood is known as the world capital of the film industry, most of the studios are now in the hands of television companies. The footprints and palm-prints of the stars, set in the concrete outside *Mann's Chinese Theater* (6925 Hollywood Boulevard), serve as reminders of the glittering past. Movie buffs can take one of the guided bus tours through Hollywood and Beverly Hills where the film idols of today have their palatial villas. The ABC, CBS and NBC television studios are also open to the public. *38/39*

JOSHUA TREE NATIONAL MONUMENT
④. This extensive national park in southern California has two main entrances: one to the north, near Twenty-Nine Palms on the S 62, and the other to the south, at Cottonwood Springs on the I 10. It offers impressive views of the desert landscape, with a wide range of

intriguing geological features and numerous species of exotic vegetation, including the bizarrely formed Joshua tree which is peculiar to the region. There is a campsite offering basic accommodation which can be booked in advance by contacting the Superintendent, Joshua Tree National Monument, 74485 National Monument Drive, Twenty-Nine Palms, CA, USA, 92277-3597, tel.: 619-367-7511. *37*

LAKE TAHOE ⑤. Nestling in a valley between the Sierra Nevadas and the Carson Mountains, Lake Tahoe is the largest and most impressive of California's mountain lakes. Approximately one-third of the lake belongs to the adjoining state of Nevada; in the 1960s, California and Nevada established a joint body to supervise the tourist trade and to protect the area from environmental damage. The deep-blue water of Lake Tahoe is still relatively clear. Among the recommended beaches are *Camp Richardson* and *Emerald Bay,* both on S 89 along the western shore.

LASSEN VOLCANIC NATIONAL PARK
⑥. Located in northeastern California at the point where the Cascade Range intersects with the Sierra Nevadas, this

spectacular national park can be approached by taking either S 36 or S 89, both of which lead off from I 5. *Lassen Peak* (10,457 feet/3,187 metres) is a giant volcano which reached a peak of activity between 1914 and 1917; since then it has remained more or less dormant. The volcanic character of the area is underlined by the ubiquitous sight of smaller volcanoes, rivers of solidified lava, hot springs and bubbling vats of grey mud. The Visitor Centre is located at the western entrance, near the junction of S 44 and S 89. Further information can obtained from the Superintendent, Lassen Volcanic National Park, PO Box 100, Mineral, CA, USA, 96063-0100, tel.: 916-595-4444.

LAVA BEDS NATIONAL MONUMENT

⑦. A collection of ancient lava formations in northeastern California, only a few miles from the Oregon border. The landscape has a lunar appearance, with deep craters and caves everywhere, and huge cylindrical pillars of lava rearing up vertically from the ground. The caves were used as a fortress and hiding-place by the Modoc Indians during their final struggle against the American army in 1872–1873. Geological and historical information about the park is available at the Visitor Center, tel.: 916-667-2282. *35*

LOS ANGELES ⑧ has both the largest

area (465 square miles/1,204 square kilometres) and the largest population (3,536,800) of any California city. Together with the southernmost part of California, Los Angeles is almost a world unto itself, with a lifestyle all of its own. The city is a conglomeration of separate districts connected by a grid of freeways, and the pace of life is dictated entirely by the automobile. The *Greater Los Angeles Visitor and Convention Bureau* (515 S. Figueroa Street, tel.: 213-624-7300) is located in the downtown area, across the street from the Arco Plaza. From here, one can walk to *Los Angeles City Hall* at 200 N. Spring Street (tel.: 213-485-4423). Completed in 1928, the building was the only one allowed to exceed the thirteen-storey limit imposed by the city authorities, a restriction which remained in effect until 1957. Close by, *Union Station* is well worth a visit: built in the Spanish mission style, it has a particularly impressive waiting-room with a ceiling nearly

Bumpass Hell, in Lassen Volcanic National Park.

fifty feet/fifteen metres high. **Exposition Park,** in the area bordered by Figueroa Street, Exposition Boulevard, Menlo Avenue and Martin Luther King Jr. Boulevard, contains several other points of interest, including the *Memorial Coliseum,* where the Olympic Games were staged in 1932 and 1984, the *California State Museum of Sciences and Industry,* and the *Natural History Museum of Los Angeles County.* The *via triumphalis* of Los Angeles is **Wilshire Boulevard,** running westward for over thirty miles/fifty kilometres from the city centre to the Pacific Ocean, via Beverly Hills and

The Los Angeles County Museum of Art.

Santa Monica. The most remarkable section of the boulevard is *Miracle Mile,* between La Brea and Fairfax Avenue: apart from the Bullock's-Wilshire department store, a fine specimen of Art Deco architecture built in 1929, the main attractions of this area are the *George C. Page Museum of La Brea Discoveries* and the *Rancho La Brea Tar Pits,* with its extensive collection of ice age fossils. For anyone interested in art, a visit to the *Los Angeles County Museum of Art* is a must. Guided tours (tel.: 213-825-4574) are available around the impressive campus of the *University of California at Los Angeles* in Westwood. Northwest of the city centre, at the junction of the Golden Gate Freeway (I 5) and Ventura Freeway (S 134), *Griffith Park* offers a chance to roam in green surroundings, and to visit the *Los Angeles Zoo,* a carefully-planned and attractive modern zoo. *40, 44/45.*

MALIBU. Located on S 1 between the Santa Monica Mountains and the Pacific Ocean, Malibu is the home of the *J. Paul Getty Museum.* Built in the style of a Roman villa, the museum has a magnificent collection of art from all ages.

MONTEREY ⑨. Formerly the capital of the Spanish-Mexican province known as Alta California, Monterey (on S 1) is a harbour town on the northern side of the Monterey Peninsula. Its erstwhile politi-

Old Sacramento State Historic Park.

cal and economic significance having dwindled, the town turned to tourism for its source of income and has made a successful job of exploiting a colourful past. The range of carefully restored historical monuments extends from the *Monterey Presidio,* a fort built in 1770 by the Spanish colonist Gaspar de Portolá, to *Cannery Row,* the street commemorated by John Steinbeck in his novel of the same name. *Monterey Historic State Park* features a Mexican *Custom House* built in 1827, and the *Monterey Aquarium,* one of the largest aquaria in the world. **Seventeen-Mile Drive,** which runs along the ocean from west Monterey to Carmel, offers an opportunity to explore the coastline. *2*

MUIR WOODS NATIONAL MONUMENT
on the southern slopes of Mount Tamalpais, seventeen miles/twenty-seven kilometres north of San Francisco, is the most accessible and also the most spectacular of California's redwood parks. Some of the sequoia trees are estimated to be seventeen hundred years old.

OAKLAND ⑩ (pop. 376,700) lies on the
eastern side of San Francisco Bay. It is linked to the city by the Bay Bridge which was opened in 1936. There are nine regional parks in the surrounding area offering many landscapes for strolling. Oakland's *Mormon Temple* at 4770

Mendocino on the north coast.

Lincoln Avenue is a conspicuous example of modern religious architecture. The *Oakland Museum,* at the junction of 10th and Oak Streets, has an interesting collection of exhibits relating to the art, culture and natural history of California. In the downtown area of Oakland, modern skyscrapers strikingly contrast with carefully-restored Victorian streets.

PASADENA is situated northeast of Los
Angeles. Huge crowds of spectators flock to the town on New Year' Day for the annual Rose Parade and the Rose Bowl football game. Pasadena is also the home of the California Institute of Tech-

nology: one of the departments of this world-famous institution is the Jet Propulsion Laboratory where the spaceship Voyager was built. The *Norton Simon Museum of Art,* at the junction of Colorado Boulevard and Orange Grove Boulevard, has a fine collection of art ranging from the early Renaissance to the mid-twentieth century.

PINNACLES NATIONAL MONUMENT.
The rock formations giving this area its name can be seen from some distance away, as one drives through Salinas Valley along US 101. There are two approach roads to the park: S 146 from the west leads directly through the brightly-coloured volcanic "pinnacles", or S 25 from the east. Drivers should note that the two roads are not connected: they both come to a dead end in the middle of the park. The Visitor Center (tel.: 408-389-4485) is located at the east entrance. The remarkable yellow sandstone formations, shaped by various types of erosion over countless millenia, stand out like castles and fortresses against the clear blue sky.

POINT REYES NATIONAL SEASHORE, an
impressive coastal landscape, with cliffs, sand-dunes and beaches, offers a chance to see the rich variety of animal and plant life on the edge of the Pacific Ocean. The Point Reyes lighthouse, built in 1870, is a conspicuous landmark. There is a Visitor Center near Olema. Enquiries should be addressed to the Superintendent, Point Reyes National Seashore, Point Reyes, CA, USA, 94956.

SACRAMENTO ⑪ (pop. 374,600) is the
state capital of California. The city is closely linked with the story of the Gold Rush: it is only a short distance from Coloma (see p.50), the place where the first gold nuggets were found in 1848. The historic district known as *Old Sacramento,* featuring museums, shops and restaurants, has been restored in the style of the nineteenth century. One of the city's principal landmarks is the dome of the *State Capitol,* built in 1870; the building is situated between L and N Streets, at the junction of 10th Street and Capitol Mall. *Sutter's Fort,* at the junction of 27th and L Streets, is a reconstructed monument to the pioneering days of the nineteenth century.

Balboa Park in San Diego.

SAN DIEGO ⑫. With a population of 1,130,000, San Diego is California's second largest city. Its origins date back to 1769, the year Spanish colonists built the Presidio fort and the mission of San Diego de Alcalá. With its ideal climate, San Diego has grown into a major commercial centre and it is remains popular with holiday-makers. *Balboa Park*, at the northwest end of the commercial district, is a large area of green parkland with numerous attractions, including museums devoted to the arts, natural history, social sciences and technology, as well as excellent sports facilities. The park is also home to the San Diego Zoo, one of the largest in the world, with its particularly fascinating sections showing tropical and subtropical species in near natural habitats. *Cabrillo National Monument* at Point Loma, commemorating the discovery of San Diego Bay by Juan Rodriguez Cabrillo in 1542, offers fine views of the city and harbour. *43*

SAN FRANCISCO ⑬ has a population of 726,000, making it the state's fourth largest city. Although its former glories have been somewhat tarnished, it is still widely regarded as *the* Californian city. It owes part of its reputation to a uniquely beautiful location, at the Golden Gate which leads into the San Francisco Bay. The hills, especially the *Twin Peaks, Telegraph Hill, Nob Hill* and *Russian Hill*, offer remarkable views of

Above: San Diego, an attractive centre for shopping and recreation.
Below: Windmills in the hilly region east of San Francisco.

the city and its surroundings. Although the Spanish Presidio and the Mission of San Francisco de Asís were built as early as 1776, the city only began to flourish in the wake of the Gold Rush. From the beginning of the twentieth century, the surrounding area became increasingly built-up. The area known as *Chinatown*, centred around Grant Avenue between Pacific Avenue and Bush Street, is almost a world unto itself. At 17 Adler Place, there is small museum devoted to the history and culture of the Chinese community. *9, 10, 11, 13, 14/15, 41*

Golden Gate National Recreation Area lies north of the Golden Gate Bridge, a structure completed in 1936. Established in 1972 to preserve the natural beauty of

the coastline, the recreation area also incorporates stretches of parkland in the north and west of the city, as well as *Alcatraz Island,* the site of the notorious maximum-security jail where big-time criminals such as Al Capone were imprisoned. There is an information centre in *Fort Mason,* at the junction of Buchanan Street and Marina Boulevard, tel.: 415-556-0560. *6/7*

Golden Gate Park, which extends between the western suburbs and the Pacific Ocean, also offers a large number of attractions. Near the eastern entrance, the *California Academy of Sciences* features a museum of natural history, an aquarium and planetarium. The nearby *M.H. De Young Memorial Museum* has an excellent collection of American art from the colonial period to the present day; the west wing of the building houses the Asian Art Museum, with its extensive collections of paintings, sculptures, ceramics and jade. A short walk from here, there is a *Japanese Tea Garden*. The Conservatory of Flowers and the Strybing Arboretum are also worth a visit. North of Golden Gate Park, the California Palace of the Legion of Honor in Lincoln Park has a superb collection of French art. From here, one also has an excellent view of the Golden Gate.

The centre of San Francisco is relatively compact, and one can walk through it with relative ease. One of its particular attractions is the *Civic Center,* in the area between Market Van Ness Avenue and McAllister Street. Grouped around the Civic Center Plaza, one finds City Hall, the Louis M. Davies Symphony Hall, War Memorial Opera House and the Veterans' Memorial Building.

SAN JOSE ⑭**,** at the southern end of San Francisco Bay, is California's third largest city (pop. 791,600). Founded in 1777, it was one of the earliest Spanish settlements. The *San Jose Historical Museum,* at the junction of Center Road and Phelan Avenue, has an extensive collection of exhibits relating to the Indian, Spanish and Mexican influences on the culture of the Santa Clara Valley. With the growth of the computer industry in the Silicon Valley, San Jose has recently risen in prominence as a major centre of state-of-the-art technology.

SAN LUIS REY DE FRANCIA. Situated between Los Angeles and San Diego, west of Oceanside on S 78, this Spanish mission, founded in 1798, is probably the most attractive and best-preserved example of mission architecture.

SAN MARINO, northeast of Los Angeles, is the home of the *Huntington Library and Art Gallery,* (1151 Oxford Road), one of the world's finest collections of rare books and manuscripts. Its many precious exhibits include a Gutenberg Bible and the hand-written manuscript of Benjamin Franklin's autobiography.

SAN SIMEON, on S 1, about forty miles/sixty-four kilometres northwest of San Luis Obispo, is the site of the *Hearst*

Above: The Conservatory of Flowers in Golden Gate Park, San Francisco.
Below: Cloister in the Mission Santa Barbara, founded in 1786.

San Simeon Historical Monument, the palatial castle built by the newspaper tycoon William Randolph Hearst, with its accompanying guest-houses and extensive grounds. The castle stands on a hill known as La Cuesta Encantada ("The Enchanted Slope"), which affords magnificent views of the surrounding landscape. Hearst's extensive collections of art and antiques are housed in the central complex. Guided tours are available and should be booked well in advance: contact MISTIX, PO Box 85705, San Diego, CA, USA, 92138-5705. There is also a Visitor Center, tel.: 805-927-2020.

SANTA BARBARA ⑮**,** on US 101, northwest of Los Angeles, is one of Cali-

fornia's most popular coastal resorts. Nestling between the Santa Ynez Mountains and the sea, it is beautifully situated; the town also has a long and colourful history. Its architectural attractions include the County Court House at 1100 Anacapa Street, built in a Moorish-influenced Spanish style in 1929. The *Mission Santa Barbara,* at the junction of Los Olivos and Laguna Streets, dates back to 1786; it is known as the "Queen of the Missions". *40*

SANTA CATALINA ISLAND ⑯**.** Separated from Los Angeles by the San Pedro Channel, this beautiful offshore island can be reached by plane or boat: private cars are not allowed outside the harbour

In Yosemite National Park.

at Avalon. Journey times are fifteen minutes by air or two hours by sea. With its striking coastline and varied sporting facilities, it is a popular place for excursions. Cycling permits can be obtained from the Conservancy, tel.: 213-510-1421. Enquiries about camping, for which a permit is also required, should be addressed to the Los Angeles County Department of Parks and Recreation, PO Box 1133, Avalon, CA, USA, 90704, tel.: 213-510-0688.

SANTA CRUZ ⑰, on S 1 south of San Francisco, on the road leading to *Monterey Peninsula*, has particularly attractive beaches and recreation facilities. The *Santa Cruz Beach Boardwalk*, located between S 1 and the beach, offers a wide variety of amusements. The beautifully situated campus of the *University of California at Santa Cruz* is also well worth visiting.

SEQUOIA and **KING'S CANYON NATIONAL PARKS** ⑱. Located in the eastern part of the state, to the south of Yosemite National Park, these two adjoining parks extend from the foothills of the Sierra Nevadas in the San Joaquin Valley to the peaks of the range, such as *Mount Whitney* (14,495 feet/4,417 metres), the highest mountain in California.

Sequoia National Park contains California's largest continuous area of redwood forest, with some of the biggest examples of these mammoth trees. The best way of getting a general overall view of the region is to take the scenic route known as General's Highway, running for forty-six miles/seventy-five kilometres from S 198 at Ash Mountain, via Giant Forest, and meeting up with S 180 at Grant Grove; this route provides the only access to *King's Canyon National Park*. King's Canyon, a narrow valley framed on both sides by huge walls of rock, is a remarkably impressive sight. Enquiries may be addressed to the main headquarters of the parks at Ash Mountain on S 198, tel.: 209-565-3341.

YOSEMITE NATIONAL PARK ⑲, on the western slopes of the Sierra Nevadas, is an area of quite extraordinary natural beauty. Apart from the scenic wonders of *Yosemite Valley*, its outstanding features include *Glacier Point, Hetch-Hetchy Reservoir*, the *Mariposa Grove of Big Trees, Tuolumne Meadows* in the High Sierras, and the *Wawona Basin*. Yosemite Village stands at the northern end of the John Muir Trail, named after the Scottish naturalist who promoted the foundation of the park. The trail leads through the Sierra Mountains to Mount Whitney at the southern end of the range.

There are several entrances to the park. The western section can be explored by taking S 140 from Merced or S 41 from Fresno. Further north, S 120 leads straight through the Yosemite Valley. From the east, turning off from US 395, it is possible to take S 120 through Tioga Pass. Information about the park can be obtained at the Visitor Center in Yosemite Village, where there is also a museum of Indian culture with exhibits relating to the history of the Miwok and Paiute Indians. *18, 21*
For recorded bulletins on weather and road conditions, call 619-873-6366 or 209-372-4605. Information about camping and recreation facilities is available from 209-372-4845.

LIST OF SOURCES AND ILLUSTRATIONS

American Indian Centre, "Proclamation to the Great White Father (1969)", in *This Country was Ours*. New York: Harper & Row, 1972.
Simone de Beauvoir, *America Day by Day*. Trans. Patrick Dudley. London: Gerald Duckworth & Co. Ltd., 1952. (*L'Amerique au Jour le Jour*. Paris: Editions Paul Morihien, 1950).
John Walton Caughy, *The California Gold Rush*. California: University of California Press, 1948.
Alonzo Delano, *Life on the Plains and Among the Diggings*. New York: 1854.
Carey McWilliams, *Southern California Country*. New York: Duell, Slon & Pearce, 1946.
Max Miller, "Writer in Hollywood", in *It Must be the Climate*. New York: Robert M. McBride & Co., 1941.
Mark Twain, *The Innocents at Home*. London: Chatto & Windus, 1906.
Stewart Edward White, "My Ming Collection", in *Speaking for Myself*. New York: Doubleday, Doran & Co. Inc., 1921.

We would like to thank all copyright holders and publishers for their kind permission to reprint. Those we were not able to reach are asked to contact us.

The map on page 48 was drawn by Christine Hartl.

DESTINATION CALIFORNIA
WINDSOR BOOKS INTERNATIONAL, 1992

©1991 by Verlag C.J. Bucher GmbH
Munich and Berlin
Translation: John Ormrod
Editor: Karen Lemiski
Anthology: Carmel Finnan
All rights reserved
Printed and bound in Germany
ISBN 1 874111 06 5